THE NUDES

A Pictorial Celebration of the Sphynx

By Chanel Jennifer Bevell

BLYSSTER PRESS

Email the author at:

Website: www.thenudesphynx.com
Facebook: www.facebook.com/chanel.bevell

"THE NUDES - A PICTORIAL CELEBRATION OF THE SPHYNX" Printing History
Blysster Press paperback edition October 2010

Blysster Press
A new kind of publisher for a new kind of world

ISBN 978-0-9826818-2-4

Printed in the United States of America
www.blysster.com

Preface

Being an avid Sphynx lover has made me search far and wide for Sphynx related gear, from artwork and jewelry to clothing and more. Other Sphynx owners will know how hard the search can be and relate to how frustrating it is to come up empty handed. Hopefully time will bring us many more options.

On one particular trip to the bookstore, I decided I was going to find a Sphynx picture book, and proudly display it to the many people who find them unattractive or even repulsive; I felt that a few camera phone photos of my cherished nakeds just weren't enough to convey just how magnificent these cats are! I could not find a book, went home and vented to my Mom. My Mom asked, "Well, why don't you do one yourself? You have 6 willing subjects at home to start with!" The idea resonated with me and I realized, yes, this was exactly what I had to do! I figured there had to be other Sphynx obsessed people out there wanting something like this book as well. I got online that night and started looking for Sphynx owners who wanted to help out. I am still amazed at the outpouring of love and support I have received. It must be the extra love our Sphynx give us coming full circle. Some people gladly offered up photos of their beautiful nakeds. Some offered to help in any way they could, even to go so far as publishing this book, and all wished me luck! It was wonderful to have so many people from the community come together and help create something beautiful. Thank you so much, each and every single one of you!

Special thanks to all of the wonderful people who have shared their beloved kitties with me, and the rest of the world. Thank you for your submissions and support. You are the heart and soul of this book. Thank you, Charity, from Blysster Press, for believing in me and this project enough to spend hours at a time making my dream a reality. You inspire me daily! Thank you to my Husband who logged as many hours in front of the computer as I did, making sure the layout was just right! Thanks to Halo Precision Piercing (www.halopiercing.com) and Arizona Hi-Fi (www.tubeaudio.com) for all of your support in the making of this book! My apologies to those I may have forgotten in the rush to get this done in time.

I hope you enjoy these photos as much as I do, and appreciate that I have not touched up any of them. Each photo, professional, straight-up-amateur, captures the very essence of the Sphynx breed. The true beauty of this breed is the amazing diversity, depth, richness and complexity each individual Sphynx's personality has. Sphynx are the most loving breed I have ever had the pleasure of meeting and knowing.

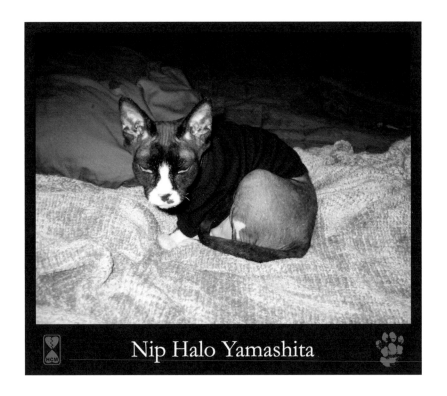

Nip Halo Yamashita

Nip was a rescue kitty, adopted from the Humane Society during a Black Cat Halloween Adoption Special. She came from a "Collector's" home. She was one of three survivors out of over **30** Sphynx. Emaciated and mistreated she still had it in her heart to bond instantly with Kelsey. As a "Special Needs" cat she blossomed and continued to fill her world with more love. Nip's condition stabilized and she led a well deserved fairly normal life for several years until her state of health started to decline. Soon after Nip passed on to a better place due to HCM. The memories of her suffering and the helplessness felt by her loved ones will never dissipate but have given inspiration and a hope to eradicate HCM so no other Sphynx or their loved ones will ever have to experience such tragedy due to HCM ever again. Nip's magnetic personality sparked a love for the Sphynx Breed in many people, even ones who never formally met her. Undoubtably, through this book, she will continue to not only touch many hearts but continue to make this world a better place.

"She was my little shadow that never left my side from the first day
when I adopted her until the day she passed away."
Kelsey Yamashita

This book is for Nip, the cat with the biggest heart in the world, and to all other kitties who's lives have been taken by this horrible disease.

WHAT IS HCM
by Brooke Arnold

As you venture into the wonderful world of the Sphynx cat, you will undoubtedly begin to see three little letters over and over again. Whether you are in the market for your first Sphynx, or if you have already become a full-blown, card carrying, naked cat fanatic, *you need to know about HCM.*

Okay then, what is HCM?

Hypertrophic Cardiomyopathy, more commonly referred to as "HCM", is the most common heart disease among cats. Let's break the phrase down to better understand what it means: "Hypertrophic" is the abnormal enlargement of an organ. "Cardio" means heart, "Myo" means muscle, and "Pathy" means disease. So, "Hypertrophic Cardiomyopathy" is basically a heart muscle disease in which the walls of the left ventricle thicken. Page after page has been written on how long most cats will live with the disease, but…cats don't know how to read!

HCM has many different factors, and no two cases are identical. An HCM cat's prognosis will vary depending on any number of things: How early the diagnosis is made, how advanced the disease is, how quickly it is progressing. Some cats will live well into their teens, unaware of any heart disease, while others are ripped away from us long before they see their second birthday. Some may be lucky enough to slip gracefully in the night. Others may have to be put down to ease the screaming pain of a blood clot, or to end the suffering as they gasp for their final breath of air.

There are several breeds that are targeted as being predisposed to HCM - including our beloved Sphynx - and research indicates HCM is passed genetically. The cardiologist will diagnose HCM using an echocardiogram, or ultrasound, of the heart.

Tell me about this echocardiogram thing.

An echocardiogram is the most conclusive means of diagnosing HCM. This allows the cardiologist a means to see and measure the walls of the heart, the size of the atrium, the condition of the valves, and if there are any blood clots present. A heart scan with an echo is the gold standard for diagnosing ,or ruling out, HCM. A board-certified cardiologist is most qualified to interpret an echocardiogram.

So, should I have my Sphynx scanned?

You should follow the advice of your veterinary cardiologist. If you're using your cat for breeding, they should be scanned by echocardiogram at least every year. If the cat has relatives, parents or siblings who are positive for HCM, you should have them scanned yearly because of the heightened risk. If you don't know the family or medical history, you should have your Sphynx scanned. If the Sphynx has any high risk factors, such as a murmur or arrhythmia, you should have them scanned. But, nearly half of cats with HCM do not have any outward signs like a murmur; so don't wait for the appearance of a murmur to have your cat scanned for HCM.

I'm looking for a Sphynx kitten

You want to know how to choose a kitten that won't develop HCM, right? Well, no one, no matter how hard they try, can guarantee that a cat will never get HCM. They can do everything within their means to avoid it...but the guarantee they offer you and the way they handle any issues that DO come up are what make all the difference in the world. Most importantly, you'll want to know if the breeder scans their breeding cats for HCM *every year*. Ask for proof! A breeder who scans their cats is proud of that fact, has paid a lot of money to do it, and will be more than willing to show you the echo reports from their board-certified cardiologist.

Find a breeder that is open and willing to discuss the topic of HCM with you, not someone who wants to change the subject or seems like they have something to hide. There are plenty of reputable breeders out there who do scan their cats and are doing their part to eradicate HCM from our breed. Secondly, try to find a breeder who offers a genetic health guarantee for longer than the typical one year. Since HCM does not present itself in most cases until mid-life, a 1-year guarantee would be worthless in the event your cat did become HCM positive later in life.

My Sphynx was diagnosed with HCM. What now?

If you haven't already, find a cardiologist you trust. Your cardiologist will guide you: Have your cat scanned often to see how the disease is progressing; make adjustments to his medications; perhaps recommend diet and lifestyle changes.

Learn everything you can about HCM. The more educated you are on the subject, the more you are able to handle the challenges. Learn how to measure your cat's respiratory rate and pulse. Learn what signs to look for in case of emergency. Know what to expect so there are no surprises.

Remember quality of life but stay hopeful. HCM is extremely unpredictable. But that means you should stay hopeful and be an advocate for your cat's heart health. Be willing to treat the disease. Medications exist that will make your companion comfortable and extend their life. As long as your Sphynx continues to fight, so should you. Cherish every moment. Love them unconditionally. Let them go if the time comes.

I want to do more!

You may not know it, but you've already helped in the fight against HCM by purchasing this book. A portion of the proceeds from the sale of each book is donated to help fund the research to find the genetic markers for HCM in Sphynx cats. With the discovery of the genetic marker, a simple cheek swab could be used to diagnose many cases of HCM. This is just one step further in ending the disease, with the hope that some day we'll never have to see those three little letters again.

Brooke Arnold is a proud Sphynx addict. She has had 7 Sphynx; one lost to HCM and one is currently surviving with it. She is a strong advocate for HCM awareness, and all of her cats are scanned yearly for the disease. She is involved with Sphynx rescue and is the Co-Administrator of a hairless cat health and wellness forum: www.sphynxforum.com

Harold by Brooke Arnold

Photos marked with the icon below are Sphynx who have HCM or have passed on from HCM. Bless their souls! This HCM Logo symbolizes, not only, the breaking heart of the Sphynx and it's family but the sand grains in an hourglass counting time trickling away for those with HCM. Let's change it!!!

A portion of the proceeds from the sale of this book will go to fund further HCM research in the Sphynx Breed. Additional donations can also be made directly to Washington State University where Dr. Kathryn Meurs is at the forefront of HCM Research:

www.vetmed.wsu.edu/deptsVCGL/index.aspx

Click the "Give Now" or "Giving Opportunities" button and direct it to Feline Cardiology.
Thank you.

Baloe Van De Noordenplassen by Sphynx Cattery Van De Noordenplassen

Baloe Van De Noordenplassen

Mrs. Cloudy's Pride Dione a.k.a. "Gummi" Van De Noordenplassen

Flora Van De Noordenplassen

Belle Van De Noordenplassen

Storm Difa Van De Noordenplassen

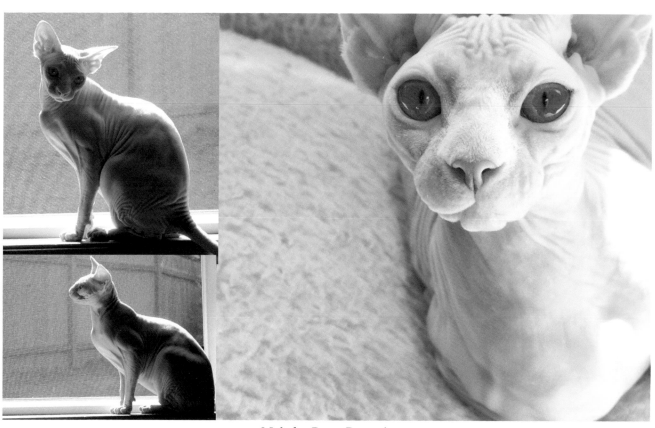

Nala by Rana Rennels

Mug-y by Alexia Charlesworth

Ducky by Erin Lacy

Ducky by Erin Lacy

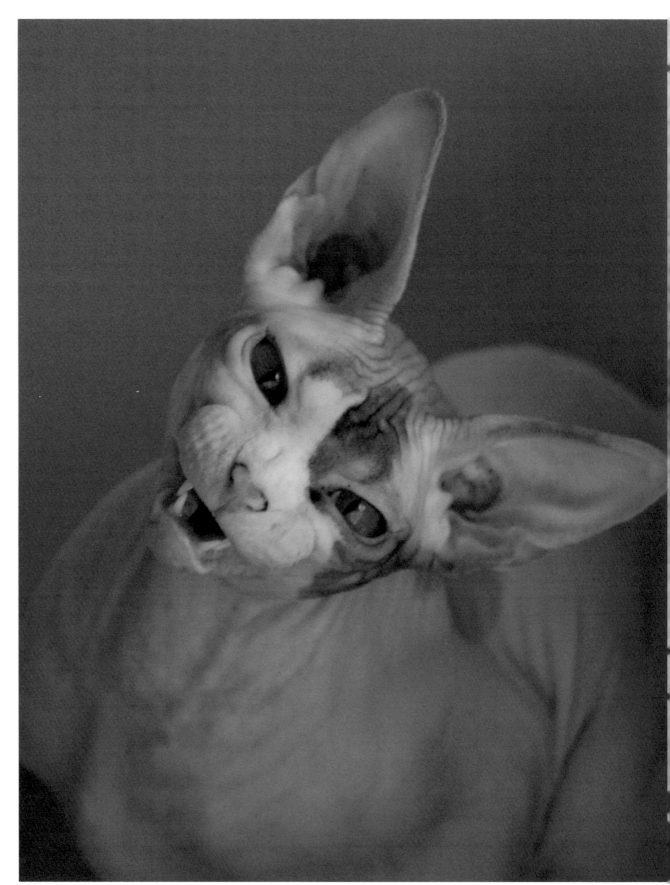

Ducky by Erin Lacy

Hibou by Holly Savage

Hibou by Holly Savage

Hibou by Holly Savage

Kokka and Hibou by Holly Savage

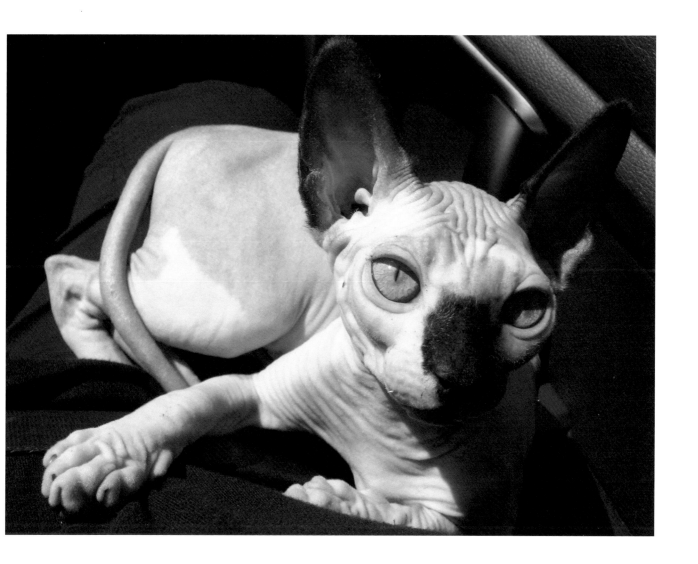

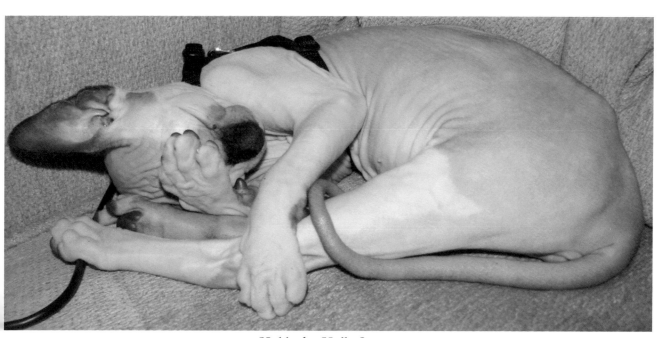

Kokka by Holly Savage

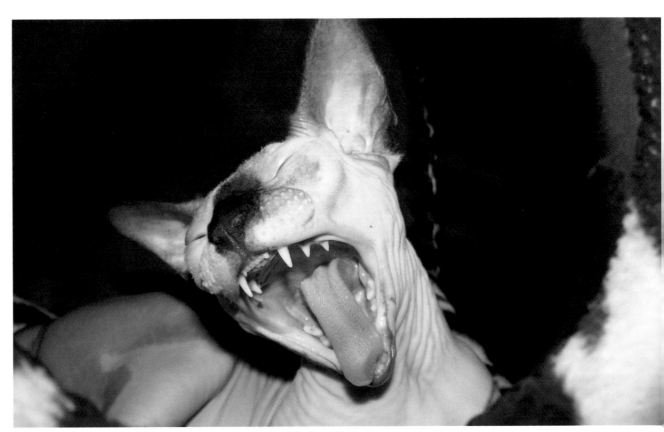

Kokka by Holly Savage

Tux and Twitch by Tess Gape

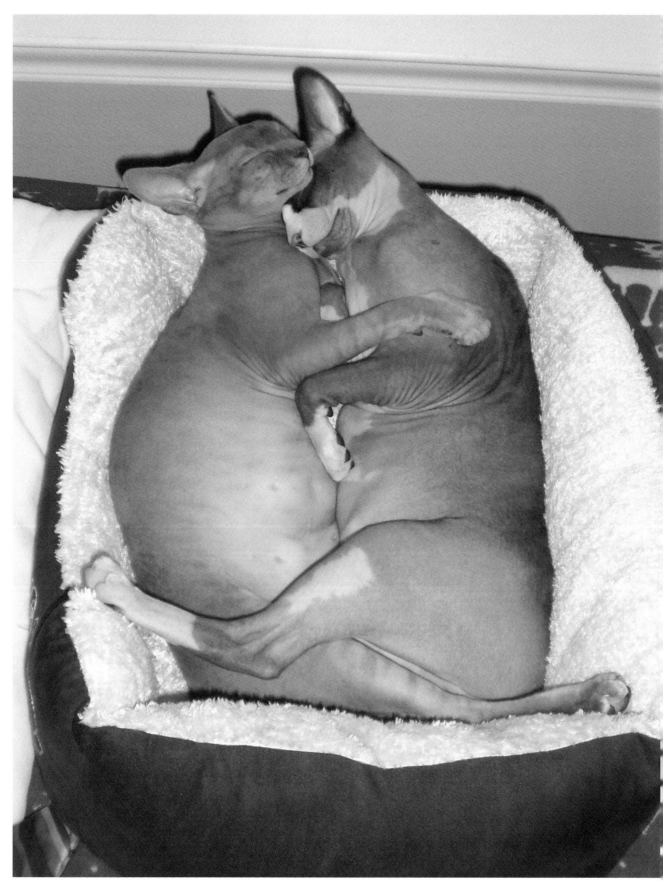

Tux and Twitch by Tess Gape

René Richter - www.sphynxeden.webnode.cz

René Richter - www.sphynxeden.webnode.cz

René Richter - www.sphynxeden.webnode.cz

René Richter - www.sphynxeden.webnode.cz

Nefertari "Neffie"

© Charity Becker
www.optycal.com

Hand-painted pet portraits by Charity Becker starting at $50 - www.optycal.com

Ariel, Jewel and Sebastian by Tracy Brennan of No Coat Kitty

Alena Yelyashovych - www.prettykitty.ru

Alena Yelyashovych - www.prettykitty.ru

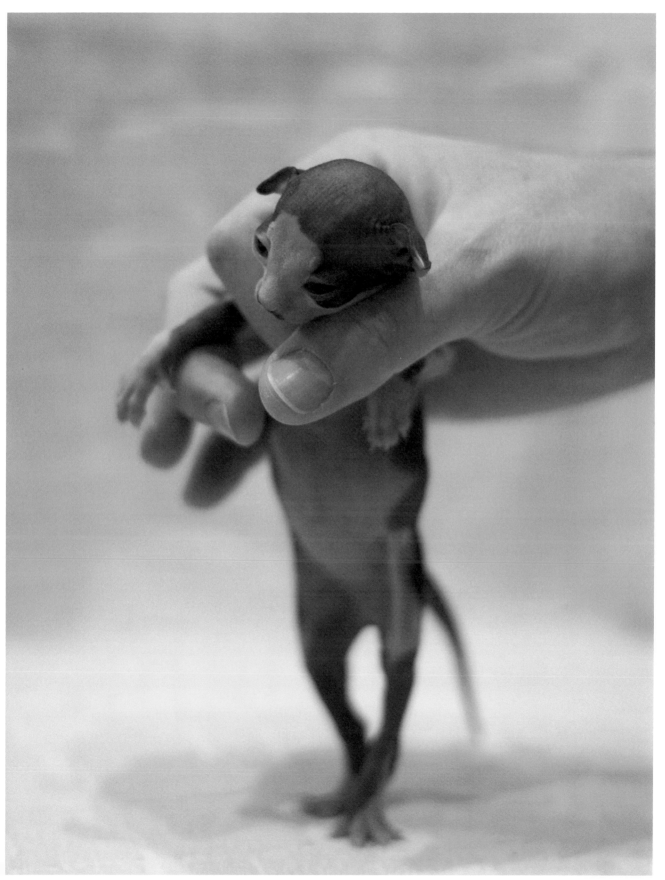

Alena Yelyashovych - www.prettykitty.ru

Alena Yelyashovych - www.prettykitty.ru

Alena Yelyashovych - www.prettykitty.ru

Alena Yelyashovych - www.prettykitty.ru

Alena Yelyashovych - www.prettykitty.ru

Alena Yelyashovych - www.prettykitty.ru

Alena Yelyashovych - www.prettykitty.ru

Cadeau and Ciel by Renee Spahr

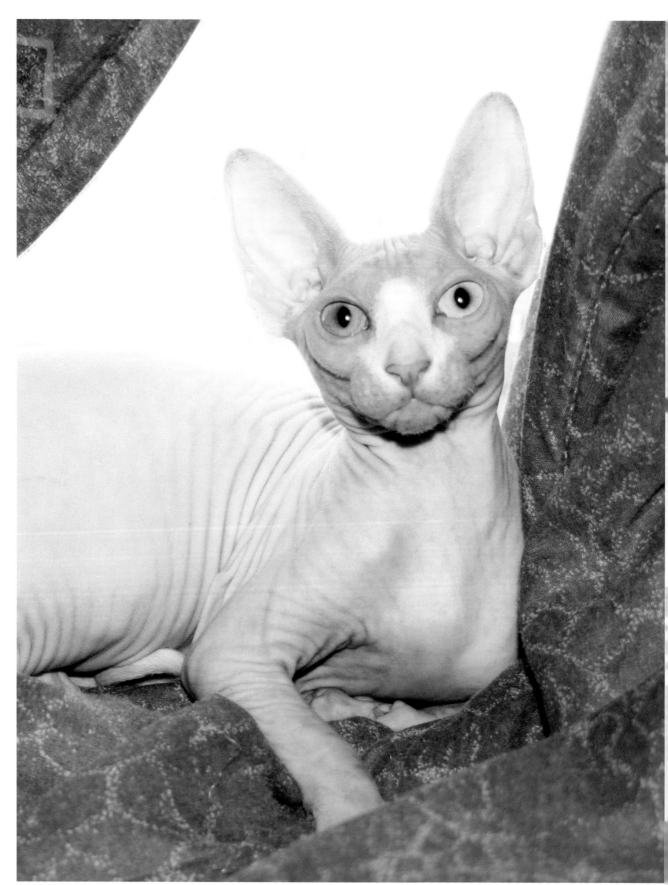

Chemere by Renee Spahr

Singe by Renee Spahr

Ra by Rona Kennedy

Dobby by Lisa Thompson-Dobo

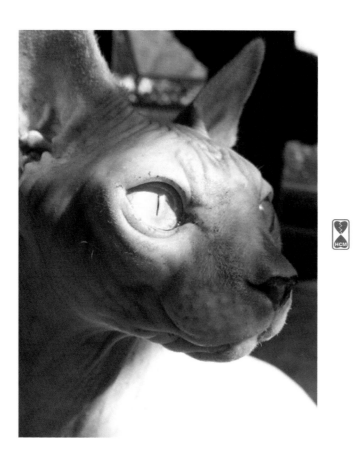

Zippy and Bella by René Laigo - www.artwichstudios.etsy.com

Nicky Ball's Misfits Sphynx photos by Chris Brignell

Nicky Ball's Misfits Sphynx photos by Chris Brignell

Nicky Ball's Misfits Sphynx photos by Chris Brignell

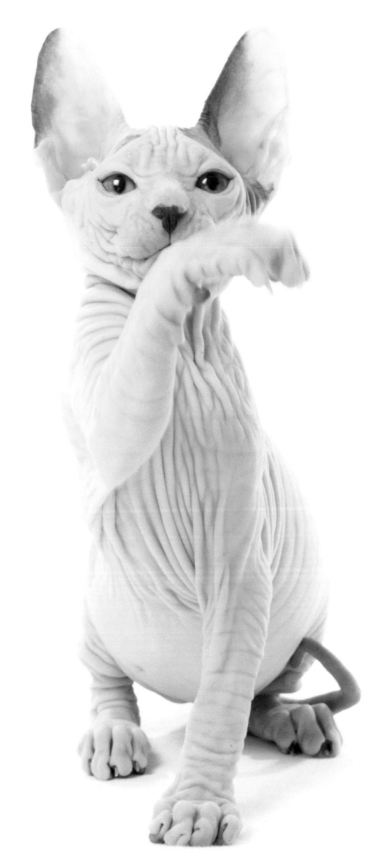

Nicky Ball's Misfits Sphynx photos by Chris Brignell

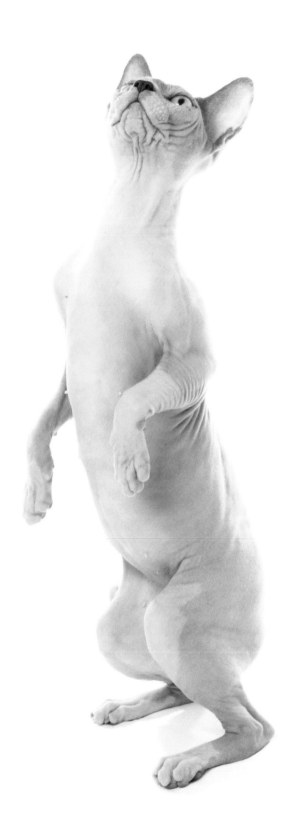

Nicky Ball's Misfits Sphynx photos by Chris Brignell

Nicky Ball's Misfits Sphynx photos by Chris Brignell

Moofin by Chanel Bevell

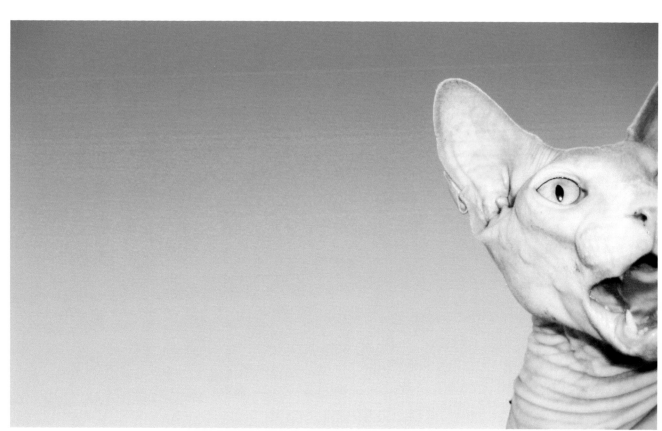

Nano and Moofin by Chanel Bevell

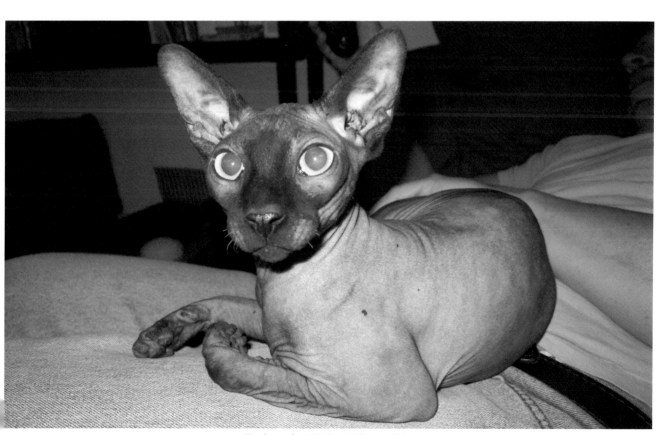

Carbon by Kelsey Yamashita

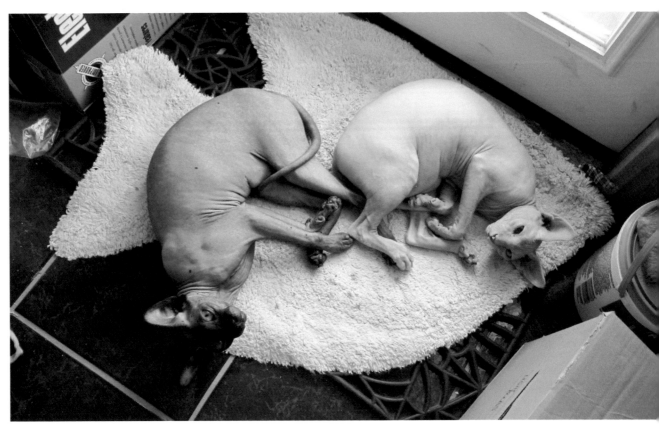

One-Eyed Jack and Carbon by Kelsey Yamashita

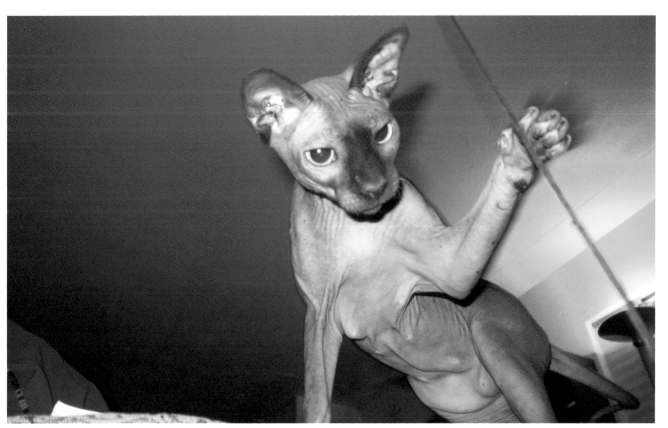

Carbonzilla by Kelsey Yamashita

Boo, Nano, Lillet, Jack and Carbon by Kelsey Yamashita

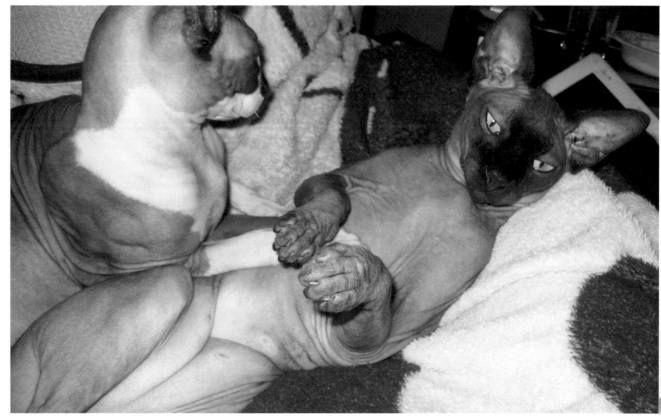

Lillet and Boo by Chanel Bevell

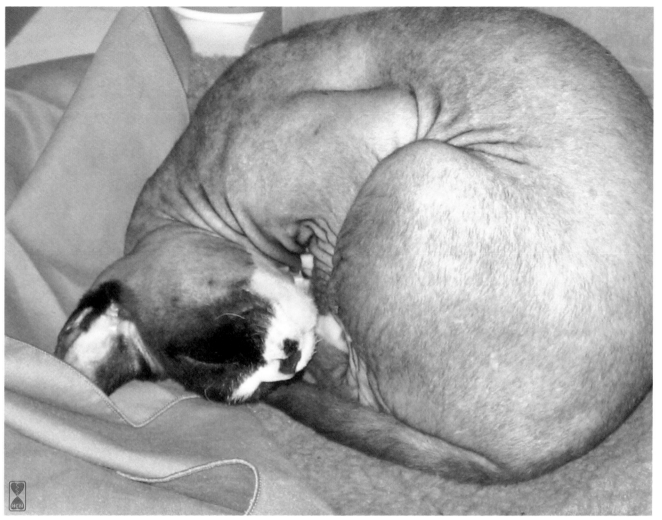

Nip by Kelsey Yamashita

Nano by Chanel Bevell

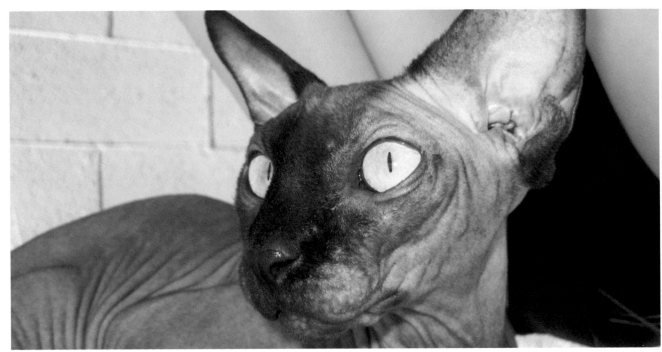

Boo by Chanel Bevell

Nano by Chanel Bevell

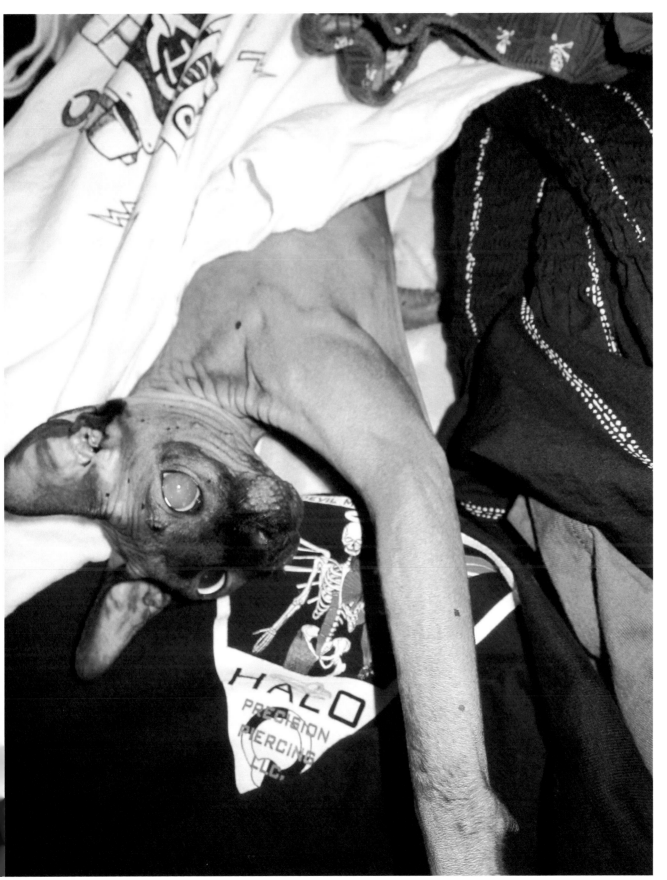

Carbon by Kelsey Yamashita

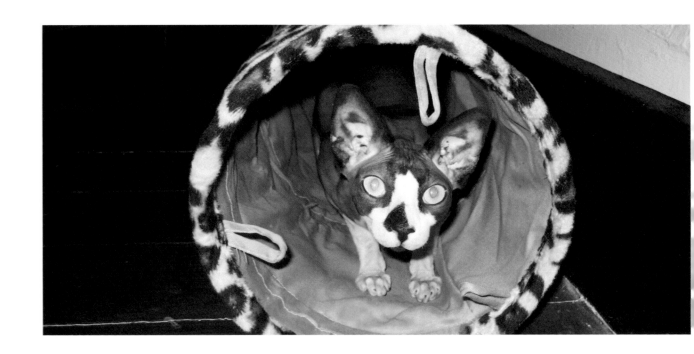

Lillet by Chanel Bevell

Moofin by Chanel Bevell

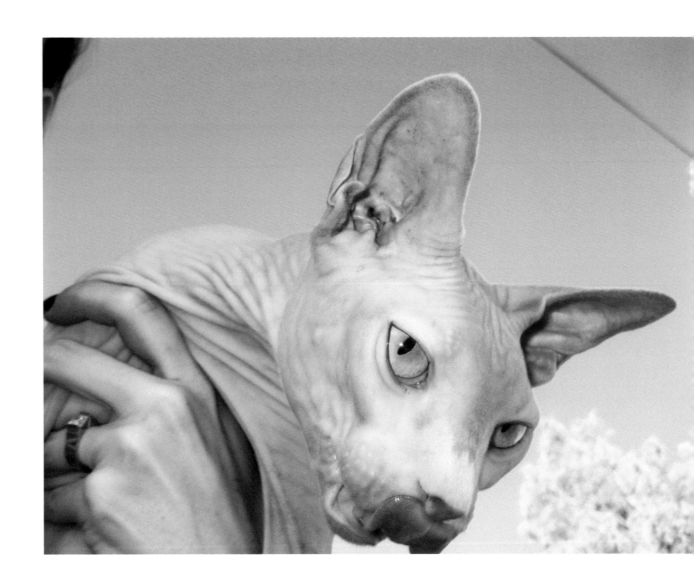

Moofin by Chanel Bevell

Nano by Chanel Bevell

Mr. Miso by Chanel Bevell

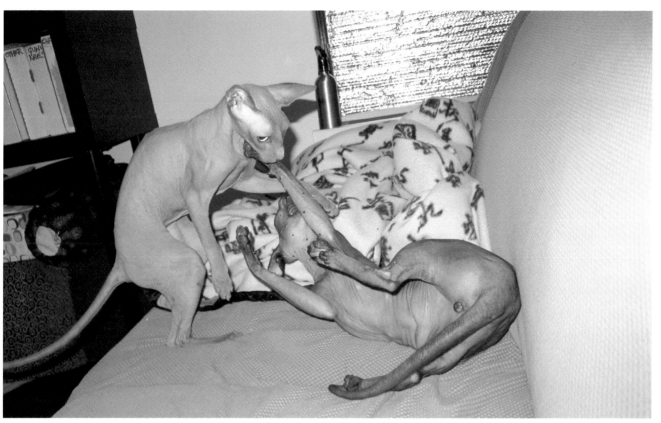

Nano and Carbon by Kelsey Yamashita

Lillet and Boo by Chanel Bevell

Mr. Miso and Nano by Chanel Bevell

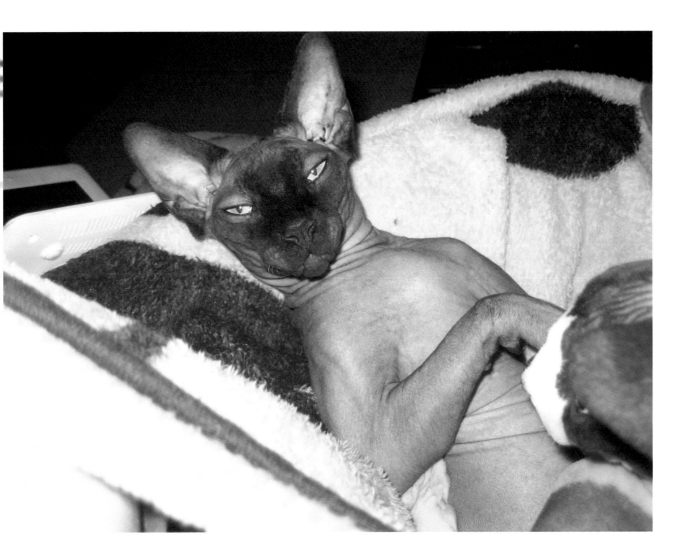

Boo, Lillet and Mr. Miso by Chanel Bevell

Carbon by Kelsey Yamashita

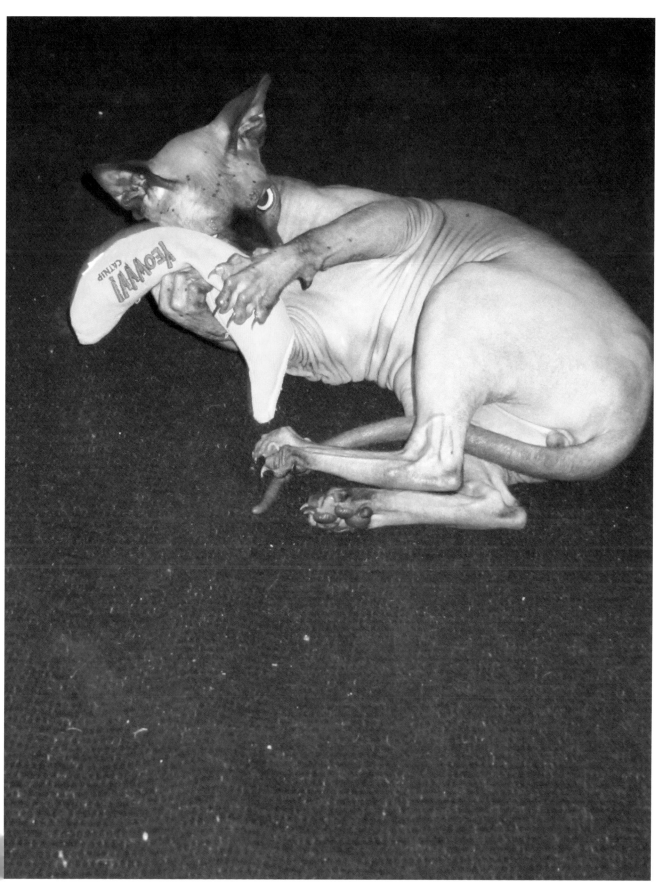

Carbon by Kelsey Yamashita

Carbon by Kelsey Yamashita

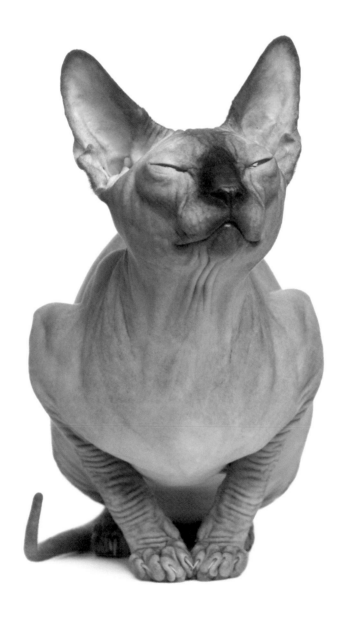

photo by Eric Isselee

photo by Dmitri Mihhailov

photo by Eric Isselee

photo by Valeriy Mazur

photo by Linn Currie

Coco and Cleo by Jacky Andersen

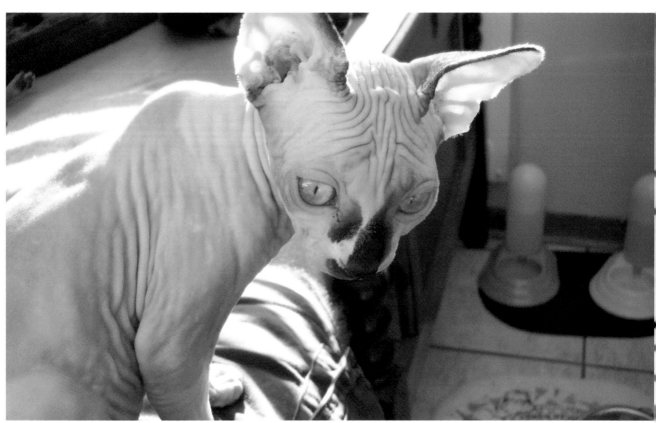

Livingstone aka "Stones" by Aurelia Williams

"Cattitude" Oil on Canvas. 24"x30" by Rene Laigo available at www.artwichstudios.etsy.com

Beeblebrox Sphynx Cattery by Desiree Bobby and Maureen Demers

Beeblebrox Sphynx Cattery by Desiree Bobby and Maureen Demers

Beeblebrox Sphynx Cattery by Desiree Bobby and Maureen Demers

Alena Yelyashovych
www.prettykitty.ru

Alena Yelyashovych
www.prettykitty.ru

Alena Yelyashovych
www.prettykitty.ru

Kokka
by Holly Savage

Zima
by Tracy Brennan of No Coat Kitty

Lulu
by Susan Meagher

One-Eyed Jack
by Chanel Bevell

Anubis
by Susan Meagher

One-Eyed Jack
by Kelsey Yanashita

Zuchini
by Susan Meagher

Pruney
by Susan Meagher

by Susan Meagher

Dulcinea
by Susan Meagher

Eden Feld
by Rene Richter - www.sphynxeden.webnode.cz

Boo
by Susan Meagher

Alena Yelyashovych
www.prettykitty.ru

Ivy
by Lisa Mayfield of www.cattitudesphynx.com

Bayleigh
by Kathy Bauman

Mr. Miso
by Chanel Bevell

Squishy
by Alison Sherrick

by René Richter - www.sphynxeden.webnode.cz

Alena Yelyashovych
www.prettykitty.ru

Kokka and Hibou
by Holly Savage

Du Reeds
by Renee Spahr

Pruney and Mabel
by Susan Meagher

Kienna and Bayleigh
by Kathy Bauman

Snuffie
by Christina Kutkuhn

Nip
by Kelsey Yamashita

Pruney
by Susan Meagher

Pruney
by Susan Meagher

Boo
by Susan Meagher

Domino and Spotty
by Susan Meagher

Coco
by Jacky Andersen

Habibi, Mabel, Othie Marie and babies
by Susan Meagher

Nefertiti
by Susan Meagher

Blue
by Kathy Bauman

Lulu, Moody and Mabel
by Susan Meagher

Snuffie
by Christina Kutkuhn

Lulu and Litter
by Susan Meagher

Snuffie
by Christina Kutkuhn

Kienna
by Kathy Bauman

Mabel
by Susan Meagher

Moody and Habibi
by Susan Meagher

Snuffie
by Christina Kutkuhn

Boo
by Susan Meagher

Lulu
by Susan Meagher

Moody and Othie Marie
by Susan Meagher

Lillet
by Chanel Bevell

Bat-Jack
by Kelsey Yamashita

Alena Yelyashovych
www.prettykitty.ru

About the Author:

Chanel Jennifer Bevell was born in Huntington Beach, California, November 01, 1980. She grew up on a farm in Santa Ynez which is where she realized her extreme affinity for all animals. Chanel currently resides in Phoenix, Arizona with her husband, Glen and the "Super Six". Mischa was the first Sphynx of the family, then Moofin. Lillet, Boo and Nano came from the same litter. Mr. Miso is from the same parents just a different litter. There are no current plans to make it the "Supreme Seven" as having Carbon and One-Eyed Jack over during Kelsey's vacations is enough fun and vice versa. Moofin and Nano are "special needs" cats. Moofin has a skin condition and Nano has extreme allergies, tests, biopsies, shots, meds and everything else involved with allergies. Allergies may very well be the next big issue for the Sphynx Breed.

Chanel can be contacted at:

www.thenudesphynx.com
www.facebook.com/chanel.bevell